The Client

JOHN GRISHAM

Level 4

Retold by Janet McAlpin
Series Editors: Andy Hopkins and Jocelyn Potter

Pearson Education Limited
Edinburgh Gate, Harlow,
Essex CM20 2JE, England
and Associated Companies throughout the world.

ISBN-13: 978-0-582-41777-9
ISBN-10: 0-582-41777-5

First published in the United Kingdom by Century Ltd 1993
This adaptation first published by Penguin Books 1996
Published by Addison Wesley Longman Limited and Penguin Books Ltd. 1998
New edition first published 1999

11

Text copyright © Janet McAlpin 1996
Illustrations copyright © David Cuzik (Pennant Illustration Agency) 1996
All rights reserved

The moral right of the adapter and of the illustrator has been asserted

Typeset by RefineCatch Limited, Bungay, Suffolk
Set in 11/14pt Monotype Bembo
Printed in China
SWTC/11

Published by Pearson Education Limited in association with
Penguin Books Ltd, both companies being subsidiaries of Pearson Plc

For a complete list of titles available in the Penguin Readers series please write to your local
Pearson Education office or contact: Penguin Readers Marketing Department,
Pearson Education, Edinburgh Gate, Harlow, Essex, CM20 2JE.

Contents

Introduction

Mark pulled a dollar from his pocket and handed it to her. 'This is all I've got.'

She put the dollar on the desk and said, 'Okay, now I'm the lawyer and you're the client. Let's hear the story.'

Mark Sway is eleven, and he knows where a body is hidden. With that body the FBI can prove a Mafia murder.

Mark wants to be honest, but he also wants to be safe. He is afraid to tell his dangerous secret because he knows that the Mafia will never forget. His younger brother is sick and his mother cannot leave the hospital. Who can he trust?

With time moving fast, Mark finds an unusual lawyer. She alone must protect the child and his family from the law and the killers. But she has help: Mark is a clever client.

John Grisham was born in 1955 in Arkansas, in the USA. He studied law, and had his own law company for nine years. He also worked in local government in Mississippi.

In 1984 he started his first book, *A Time to Kill*. He went to the office at 5 a.m. every day to write it. It took three years, but it didn't sell very well. Two years later, his next book, *The Firm*, was a best-seller, and became a film with Tom Cruise. John Grisham was able to give up law and write *The Pelican Brief*. This became another bestseller, and another film, with Julia Roberts.

John Grisham now lives on a large farm in Mississippi with his wife and two children. He is one of the world's bestselling crime writers. *The Client* is his fourth book and it has also been made into a film.

You can also read *The Firm* and *The Pelican Brief* in Penguin Readers.

Chapter 1   A Terrible Secret

School was finished and Mark had four cigarettes in his pocket. Other boys drank beer, and some tried drugs, but Mark just liked cigarettes. Now his little brother Ricky wanted his first smoke, and Mark felt terrible.

The boys walked down a narrow path into the trees behind their home. Home was a trailer in a trailer park in Memphis, Tennessee. Mom wasn't back from work yet. Dad wasn't there either. Mom left him five years ago because he was always drunk and often violent. Now Mark seemed like Ricky's father. An eleven-year-old father. He taught Ricky to play football, to ride a bike, and everything he knew about sex, but he didn't want to teach him to smoke.

'Sit there,' said Mark, when they reached his secret hiding place. 'And let's hear the rules again.'

Ricky knew them both. 'If I tell anyone, you'll hit me.'

'That's right.'

'And I can smoke only one a day.'

'That's right. If I catch you smoking more, or if you start drinking beer . . .'

'You'll hit me harder.'

'Right,' said Mark. 'Now watch me. It's really easy.'

Ricky was soon busy blowing smoke like a man. Mark sat next to him and lit another cigarette. 'I was nine when I started,' he said. 'You're only eight. You're too young.'

Ricky didn't answer. He was listening to something. Then Mark heard it too, and they stopped smoking. 'Just sit still,' Mark said softly.

Through the trees they could see an old road, which nobody used any more. A long, black car appeared on the road and came slowly across the rough ground. It made a circle, then stopped. Soon the engine stopped too.

'He's trying to kill himself,' said Mark.

Hidden in the long grass behind the car, the boys watched the car. After a few minutes a fat man got out.

'What's he doing?' Ricky whispered. The man had a rubber tube. He put one end into the tail pipe of the car, and the other end through a window. He got into the car, closed the window as tight as he could and started the engine again.

'He's trying to kill himself,' said Mark. 'I saw a man do it like this in a film once.'

'How long does it take?'

'Not very long,' said Mark, 'but I'm going to stop him.'

Mark crawled to the car, pulled away the tube and crawled back. 'Quick, let's get out of here,' said Ricky.

Suddenly the man got out of the car again. He had a bottle of whisky and a gun, and he was crying. 'Let's get out of here,' said Ricky again, urgently.

Mark watched quietly. The man looked at the tube, he looked around, then he put the tube back into the tail pipe. He got back into the car with his whisky.

'Mark, please, let's go,' said Ricky, and began to cry.

'I'll try one more time,' said Mark.

Ricky watched his brother crawl forward again, and then the man saw Mark. He fell out of the car and grabbed him. 'You little . . . ,' he shouted, as he hit Mark. 'Get into the car.' Ricky, in shock and fear, wet himself.

The man pushed Mark into the car and hit him again. Then he laughed. 'My name's Jerome Clifford – Romey to my friends. What's yours?'

'Mark,' said Mark.

Romey laughed. 'Here,' he said. 'Take the whisky, son. Let's die together.'

Mark took the bottle and pretended to drink. He smelled gas. He looked at the gun on the seat.

'We'll be dead in five minutes,' said the man.

Mark looked in the mirror and saw Ricky crawling towards the back of the car. 'Why are you doing this?' he asked.

'Give me the whisky,' said the man.

Mark looked at the man. If he gets drunk he might go to sleep, he thought. He passed the whisky.

'It's because of the body,' said the man. 'It's at my house. I'm a lawyer. My client killed a senator.* The FBI† is looking everywhere for his body and my client hid it in my garage. Can you believe it? Right there, under my boat!'

Mark smelled the air again. No gas now, thanks to Ricky. 'Who's your client, Romey?' he asked.

'Barry the Blade,' said Romey. 'He's a member of the Mafia‡ in New Orleans. Now he wants to kill me because I know about the body. But he can't because the gas will kill us first.' He laughed, and drank more whisky.

Soon he was drunk and asleep. Mark gently opened the car door and ran to where Ricky was hiding. 'I pulled the tube out,' said Ricky in a high voice.

Mark lit a cigarette and watched the car. Suddenly the door fell open and the lawyer came out with the gun in his hand. He saw the tube and started screaming. His wild red eyes looked round for Mark, but Mark was well hidden in the long grass. Then he stood still, put the gun in his mouth, closed his eyes and fired.

Ricky made a low noise, like an animal in pain, and ran.

Mark looked at the dead man and thought, 'Here's trouble.' He followed Ricky home. When he got there he called 911 for the police. He knew that every 911 call was recorded.

'There's a body on the old road behind Tucker Trailer Park on Highway 17,' he said.

* Senators, in the USA, are members of government.
† The FBI is the USA's national crime-fighting body.
‡ The Mafia is a secret crime group which began in Sicily and arranges many criminal activities in the USA.

'There's a body on the old road behind Tucker Trailer Park on
Highway 17,' said Mark.

'We need your name, son.'

Mark said nothing, and put the phone down.

Chapter 2   In Trouble with the Cops

Ricky was sick. He seemed to be crying, but there were no tears. His skin was cold and wet. His thumb was in his mouth, his eyes were open and his body was shaking.

Mark was worried. He remembered a television programme about some kids* who saw a horrible accident. After that their thumbs were in their mouths like babies for a year.

'Mark,' said his mother. 'How did you cut your face?'

Mark didn't want to lie to his mother, but he didn't want to tell her about the man with the gun either.

'It's a long story, Mom,' he said.

Dianne sighed and bit her nails. They were sitting in a small room in St Peter's hospital. She lit a cigarette and watched her younger son. When she got home from work and saw Ricky she had called the family doctor. He had called an ambulance immediately. Now they were waiting for a hospital doctor to look at Ricky.

It was past supper time and Mark was restless. He opened the door. 'I'll go and get us a hamburger, Mom,' he said.

Mark stepped outside the room and a hand grabbed him. He looked up into the face of a cop.†

'Mark Sway?' asked the cop. Mark nodded.

'We've found the body,' said the cop.

'What body?' said Mark.

'Come on Mark, we know you live in Tucker Trailer Park. You made the call, didn't you?'

Mark wanted to lie, but he said, 'Yes, sir.'

---

* 'kids' is a common word for 'children'
† 'cop' is a common word for 'policeman'

'Well Mark, let's go and get those hamburgers,' said the cop, and he took Mark down to the hospital cafe.

'How did you find the body, Mark?'

'My brother and I were playing in the trees.'

'Did you take any drugs?'

'No, sir.'

'But you were smoking,' said the cop. 'We found your dead cigarettes. Stay away from drugs, son.'

'Yes, sir.'

'Did you see the man before he shot himself?'

'No, sir.'

'So you just found him dead. Have you ever seen a dead body before?'

'Only on TV.'

The cop smiled. Kids saw everything on television these days. 'What happened to your face?' he asked.

'I got in a fight at school. The other kid started it.'

'The other kid always does. What's his name?'

'You don't know him,' said Mark.

'Well, I might want to talk to him,' said the cop. 'Now tell me, why didn't you give your name to 911?'

'I don't know.'

'Come on Mark, you must know why.'

'I don't know. Afraid, I guess.' Mark tried to look very young and innocent. 'Do you think I'm lying?'

'I don't know, kid. Your story is full of holes,' said the cop. 'I think you were there, smoking, in the trees, and I think you saw the whole thing. That's why your brother's in shock, isn't it? That's why you're afraid?'

Mark's heart stopped and his blood ran cold. He tried to seem calm. His hands were shaking so he sat on them. Things were happening too fast. Could he go to prison? Could Ricky go mad? He needed time to think.

7

'How did you find the body, Mark?'

'Eat your food now,' said the cop. 'We'd better get back to your Mom. You can bring your Coke with you.'

Chapter 3   Evidence

News of Jerome Clifford's death travelled fast to the Mafia in New Orleans. His client, Barry Muldanno, was not sorry, but he was worried.

Barry the Blade, or simply The Blade as he liked to be called, wore shiny suits and a lot of gold. Barry enjoyed a fast life, and liked people to be afraid of him. His lawyer certainly was, and that's why he killed himself.

Barry liked to spend hours on his long, black hair. His face was often in the newspapers these days, because of the trial. He had killed a senator, and his trial for murder was to take place in four weeks. Barry was not worried about the trial, because nobody could find the senator's body. Without the body, who could prove a murder?

Jerome Clifford was a good Mafia lawyer, but Barry had frightened him. He told Romey where the body was hidden. He told him the body was under Romey's own boat, in his own garage. What a joke! But then Romey had disappeared, and now he was dead. Barry needed a new lawyer quickly.

♦

Roy Foltrigg also knew about the death, and was already on his way to Memphis to find out more. He hated flying, so his car was fitted with phones and television and even a fax machine. He had a driver too, so that he could work as he travelled. He hoped to arrive in Memphis by midnight.

Foltrigg was a US government lawyer. His job was to prove that Barry Muldanno killed the senator, but where was the body?

9

Maybe there would be some evidence in Memphis. Maybe Clifford had known something, said something . . .

♦

Another man wanted to know more about Jerome Clifford's death, too. He was a crime reporter who worked on the Memphis Press. He wanted a story for the morning newspaper, and he didn't care how he got it.

Slick Moeller's real name was Alfred, but nobody knew it. Everyone called him Slick. Crime was his life. He knew everyone, talked to everyone, and never named anyone who trusted him with secrets. He often knew about a crime before the cops. He knew them all, and drank coffee with them in all-night coffee bars. He had spent the morning at their head office, and now he was in St Peter's hospital.

Slick knew there was something interesting about this death. He knew Clifford was Barry Muldanno's lawyer. He knew Roy Foltrigg was coming to town. He knew about the two boys, and that one of them was in shock. And he knew some things that Mark didn't know. Jerome Clifford had left a note which nobody could read. And there were strange fingerprints on his whisky bottle.

♦

The FBI now controlled the case. Two FBI detectives waited for Roy Foltrigg. One was Jason McThune, FBI Memphis, and the other was Larry Trumann, FBI New Orleans. They had the dead man's car and all the other evidence. They knew someone had been in the car with Jerome Clifford because there were fingerprints on the whisky bottle.

'Whose are they?' said Trumann.

'Maybe the kid's,' said McThune. 'How can we check?'

'I'll get you his Coke bottle,' said one of the cops. 'You can check that.'

Chapter 4   Lawyers and FBI Men

Mark was a thinker and a worrier. When he couldn't sleep he went for long secret walks. It started when his mother and father were fighting. He wore dark clothes and left the trailer to move like a thief through the night. He saw lovers, and he saw crime. He learned much, but he never told. He loved to sit on the hill above the trailer park and enjoy a quiet smoke. He was glad to find peace when he got home.

Now his mother and his brother were asleep in the hospital room, but Mark was still awake. He watched them sleep for twenty minutes, and then got bored. He was not afraid of strange places. He quietly covered his mother with a blanket and left the room. The hall was quiet and empty. He took the lift down to the cafe.

There were two people at one of the tables. One was in a wheel-chair. The other was offering him a white card.

'My name's Gill Teal,' he said with a big smile. 'Did you have an accident? Maybe I can help you.'

The other man didn't smile. 'Road accident,' he said. 'Two broken legs.' Mark could see he was in pain.

'Well,' said Gill Teal. 'I'm a lawyer and maybe you have a case. Who hit you?'

The other man looked at the lawyer carefully. 'It was an Exxon lorry,' he said. 'He didn't stop at a red light.'

'Great,' said Gill Teal. 'I've got money from Exxon before. What have you got – two broken legs? I can get you six hundred thousand dollars for that.'

'I talked to another lawyer today. He said he could get me a million.'

'He's lying,' said Gill Teal. 'Trust me. But maybe we can get more. Are you married? Have you got kids?'

'Three kids,' said the man. He looked tired.

'Great,' said Gill Teal. 'For a family we can get more. Five hundred a month until you get back to work. Look, choose me and you'll get the best, I promise.'

'I'll think about it,' said the man.

'Can I call you tomorrow?' said the lawyer.

'No,' said the man, 'I said I'd think about it.'

Gill Teal got up. 'OK,' he said, 'you think about it. You've got my card.' He shook hands and left.

The man in the wheelchair pushed himself away, leaving the card on the table. When he had gone Mark took the card. He looked at the name and the address. He put the card in his pocket and sat back to watch the television.

♦

Roy Foltrigg liked to be on television. He really enjoyed those moments when the cameras were waiting for him. Just at the right moment he would arrive, walking quickly, holding his hand up like a very important man who would love to answer questions but just didn't have the time. He spent many pleasant moments watching videos of himself arriving at important places. Tonight, however, there were no cameras, and no reporters when he arrived at the FBI offices in Memphis. It was after midnight.

Jason McThune and Larry Trumann introduced themselves. There was only one chair, and Foltrigg took it. McThune explained the facts quickly. He told Foltrigg about finding the car, what was in it, the gun, the time of death, and about Mark Sway. 'Mark and his younger brother found the body and told the police. They live about half a mile away in a trailer park. The younger kid is in hospital now. He's in shock. His mother, Dianne, is with him, and Mark is there too. He's lying.'

'What's he lying about?' asked Foltrigg.

'He says he arrived after Clifford shot himself, but we don't believe him,' said McThune. 'First, his fingerprints are all over the

*McThune told Foltrigg about finding the car, what was in it,
the gun, the time of death, and about Mark Sway.*

car, inside and out. They're on Jerome's whisky bottle, and they're on the tail pipe too.'

'How did you check his prints?' asked Foltrigg.

'Off a bottle of Coke he drank tonight,' said McThune. 'Next, we found three cigarettes near the car. We think the boys were having a quiet smoke when Clifford arrived. They hid and watched him. Maybe they pulled his tube from the tail pipe. We're not sure, and the kids aren't telling. The little boy can't talk just now, but we're sure Mark is lying.'

'What about Clifford?' asked Foltrigg.

'We checked his blood,' continued McThune. He was drunk, and full of drugs too. We can't know what he was thinking. We know he left New Orleans in the morning, and we think he bought the gun here in Memphis.'

'Why Memphis?'

'He was born here,' said McThune. 'Maybe he wanted to die where he was born. He left a note,' he added, picking up a piece of paper. 'It tells his secretary what to do after his death. We couldn't find the pen that wrote it.'

Foltrigg took it from him and read it. 'What's this at the bottom?' he asked. 'The ink is different. It says "Mark, Mark where are . . ." but I can't read the rest.'

'Right,' said McThune. 'We can't read that bit either. We found the second pen in the car, so maybe Clifford used it there, but he was too drunk to write clearly.'

Foltrigg listened with his mouth open. 'So what does it mean?' he asked.

'There's no Mark in Clifford's family,' said McThune. 'We checked. So we think the note is for Mark Sway. But how did he know Mark's name unless he talked to him?'

'Why would the kid lie?'

'Because he's afraid,' said McThune. 'We think he was in the car. We think he and Clifford talked about something. At some point the kid left the car. Clifford tried to add something to the note and then shot himself.'

Foltrigg's mouth was open again.

'Maybe the kid's afraid because Clifford told him something he doesn't need to know,' finished McThune.

Foltrigg shut his mouth, put the note on the desk and cleared his throat. 'Have you talked to the kid?' he asked.

'Not yet,' said McThune. 'We'll do that first thing in the morning. We'd like to talk to his little brother too, but we'll have to ask his doctor.'

'I'd like to be there,' said Foltrigg, thinking about the body. 'We must know everything Mark Sway knows.'

Chapter 5   In the Hospital

Mark was asleep in front of the television when a nurse found him next morning. She gave him some orange juice and took him to Ricky's room. 'Dr Greenway is here,' she said, 'and he wants to see you.'

Dianne looked tired. She stood at the foot of Ricky's bed and her hands were shaking. Mark stood next to her, and she put her arm on his shoulder. They watched as the doctor touched Ricky's head and spoke to him. Ricky's eyes were closed.

'He doesn't hear you, Doctor,' Dianne said finally. She didn't like the way Greenway was using baby talk. Greenway continued touching and talking. Dianne had tears in her eyes. Mark smelled fresh soap and noticed her hair was wet. She had changed her clothes too, but there was no make-up.

Greenway stood straight. 'A very bad case,' he said, staring at Ricky's closed eyes.

'What's next?' said Dianne.

'We wait,' said the doctor. 'He'll wake up, and when he does it's

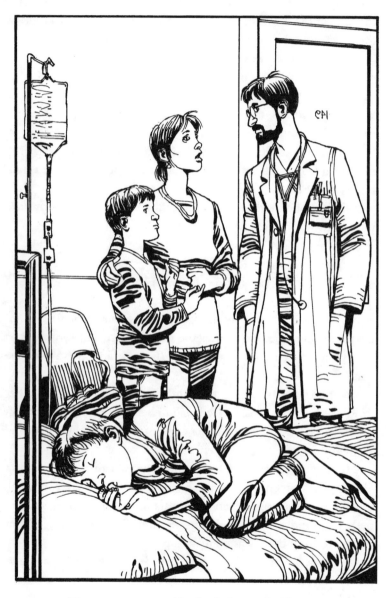

'Have you seen cases like this before?' asked Dianne.

very important that you are in this room. He must see his mother when he opens his eyes. Do you understand?'

'I'm not leaving,' said Dianne.

Greenway looked at Mark. 'You can come and go a bit, but it's best if you stay here as much as possible too.'

Mark nodded his head, but he knew he would get bored.

'Have you seen cases like this before?' asked Dianne.

Greenway looked at Ricky and decided to tell the truth. He shook his head. 'Not quite this bad,' he said. 'But I'm not worried. Ricky will be all right. It'll just take some time.' He took a card and a newspaper from his bag. 'Here's my phone number,' he said. 'If Ricky wakes up, tell the nurses and they'll call me immediately. Okay?'

Dianne took the card and nodded. Greenway opened the newspaper. 'Have you seen this?' he asked.

'No,' she answered.

'Well you'd better read it. It's about Mr Clifford.'

Mark looked at the paper and saw a big photo of Romey. Underneath the photo he read: MAFIA LAWYER SHOOTS HIMSELF. The word 'Mafia' jumped at Mark, and suddenly he felt sick.

Greenway leaned forward and spoke softly to Dianne. 'It seems that Mr Clifford was a well-known lawyer in New Orleans. He was working on a murder case. The police and the FBI are downstairs. They want to talk to Mark.'

'Why?' asked Dianne.

'It's a big case. The murdered man was a senator. You'll understand more when you read this story. Then you can talk to them.'

'No,' said Mark suddenly.

Dianne and Greenway looked at him. 'I don't want to talk to them,' said Mark. 'I – I might get like Ricky if I have to talk about it,' he added.

'Keep them away for now,' said Dianne.

'All right,' said the doctor. 'I'll keep them away until twelve. Now don't worry. Just stay by this bed until I come back.'

Greenway left. Dianne ran to the bathroom with the newspaper and lit a cigarette. Mark turned on the television by Ricky's bed and found the news programme. Nothing but weather and sports.

Dianne came back into the room. 'Clifford's client killed a United States senator,' she said slowly.

'I wonder why he did that,' said Mark, because he could think of nothing different to say.

'It says Jerome Clifford worked for the New Orleans Mafia, and they think his client is a member.'

Mark had seen film about the Mafia on television. His heart jumped, and he felt pains in his stomach.

'I'm hungry, Mom. Are you hungry?'

'Why didn't you tell me the truth, Mark?'

'I'm sorry, Mom. I planned to tell you when we were alone.'

Dianne looked sad and tired. 'You never lie to me Mark.'

'I'm really hungry, Mom. Can we talk about this later? Give me some money and I'll run down to the cafe and get us something to eat. Don't you want some coffee?'

Luckily Dianne wasn't ready for a serious talk yet. She opened her purse and gave him five dollars. Mark took the money and put it in his pocket.

'You know where the cafe is?' asked Dianne. He nodded. 'Be careful,' she said, and sat down again to watch Ricky. Mark left the room. He needed time to think.

Chapter 6   Reggie Love

As Mark ate his breakfast in the café he looked at Gill Teal's card. He knew what he needed to do. He took some coffee back to his mother and gave her a kiss.

'I'm going to look around the hospital for a bit,' he told her, and left the room again. He asked the nurses for a phone book and looked at the city map. Gill Teal's office was not far away. Then he went downstairs again and left the hospital by a back door.

Mark walked quickly. It was Tuesday and he was the only kid on the street. He didn't want anyone to ask why he wasn't at school. Gill Teal's building was old and very tall. He entered the lift with a crowd of others and went to the third floor.

When he got out he was in a long hall with a lot of doors. He tried to walk calmly, looking at the names on the doors. They were all lawyers, but he wanted Gill Teal. At the end of the hall he found the right door. The words GILL TEAL − THE PEOPLE'S LAWYER were painted on it. Three people waited by the door.

Mark entered the office. It was crowded with sad, sick people, just like the hospital. Mr Teal certainly had a lot of clients.

'What do you want?' said someone rudely.

Mark answered softly, 'I'd like to see Mr Teal.'

'Does he know you?'

'No, ma'am.'

'Did you have an accident?'

'No, ma'am.'

'Well, you're in the wrong place. Why do you need a lawyer?'

'It's private,' said Mark.

'Look, kid, you see all these people? They're all waiting to see Mr Teal. He's a very busy man, and he only takes accident cases.'

'Okay,' said Mark. He was glad to leave the crowded office. He took the stairs and walked around the second floor. More lawyers. He passed a few of them in the hall. They were too busy to notice him.

Suddenly he saw a policeman coming towards him. The next door had REGGIE LOVE − LAWYER painted on it in small letters.

19

'Hello Mark,' said the lawyer. 'I'm Reggie Love.'

Mark quickly opened the door and stepped inside. There was a glass table, some magazines, soft music, and three chairs – and nobody waiting.

A young man with a tie but no jacket sat behind a desk. 'May I help you?' he said quite pleasantly.

'I'd like to see a lawyer.'

'Aren't you a bit young?'

'Yes, but I'm having some problems. Are you Mr Love?'

'No, I'm Clint. I'm Reggie's secretary.'

'Then I need to see Reggie,' said Mark.

'What's your name?' asked the secretary.

'Mark Sway.'

'Are you in trouble, Mark?'

'Yes.'

'What type of trouble? You need to tell me a little bit about it, or Reggie won't talk to you.'

'Well,' said Mark, 'I have to talk to the FBI at twelve, and I think I need a lawyer.'

This was good enough. Clint went away for a moment, then came back. He took Mark to the lawyer's office.

'This is Mark Sway,' he said.

'Hello Mark,' said the lawyer. 'I'm Reggie Love.'

Mark looked at the lawyer in surprise. Reggie Love was a woman.

Chapter 7   Lawyer and Client

Reggie Love was fifty-two years old, and had been a lawyer for only five years. The first thing that Mark noticed about her was her hair. It was gray, and very short – shorter than his. Her eyes were green and she wore round, black glasses. Her dress was black too. She put out her hand and Mark shook it.

21

'Would you like something to drink?' she asked him.

'No, ma'am.'

She crossed her legs. 'Mark Sway, right? Please don't call me ma'am. I'm old enough to be your grandmother, but you can call me Reggie, okay?'

'Okay.'

'How old are you Mark? Tell me a little about yourself.'

'I'm eleven. I go to school at Willow Road.'

'Why aren't you in school this morning, Mark?'

'It's a long story.'

'Clint said you have to meet the FBI at twelve today. Is this true?'

'Yes,' said Mark. 'They want to ask me some questions at the hospital.'

'The hospital?' She took out a piece of paper and a pen.

'It's part of the long story. Can I ask you something, Reggie?' It was strange calling this lady by a man's name.

'Sure,' she said with a smile.

'If I tell you something, will you ever repeat it?'

'Of course not.'

'Never?'

'Only if you tell me I can repeat it. Talking with a lawyer is like talking to your doctor. What we say is secret, and held in trust. Do you understand?'

'What if I tell you something that no one but me knows?'

'I can't repeat it.'

'Something the police really want to know?'

'I can't repeat it,' she said again. 'Any more questions?'

'Yes. Where did you get the name Reggie?'

'My name used to be Regina. I was married to a doctor. Then all sorts of bad things happened and my husband left me. I changed my name to Reggie and became a lawyer.'

'My father left my mother.'

'I'm sorry.'

'Don't be sorry. My brother and I were really happy about it. He drank a lot and hit us. He hit Mom too. Me and Ricky always hated him.'

'Ricky's your brother?'

'Yes. He's the one in hospital.'

'What's the matter with him?'

'It's part of the long story.'

'Would you like to tell me this story?'

Mark was silent. He wasn't ready to talk yet.

'Are you afraid, Mark?'

'A bit. One person is dead. One is in the hospital. The police and the FBI want to talk to me.'

'Look, Mark,' she said. 'First you have to pay me something and then I'm your lawyer. I guess you don't have much money, do you?'

Mark pulled a dollar from his pocket and handed it to her. 'This is all I've got.'

She put the dollar on the desk and said, 'Okay, now I'm the lawyer and you're the client. Let's hear the story.'

Mark took a long breath and looked at the floor. He told her about Ricky and the cigarettes and the car and the man. Reggie asked questions and wrote everything down. Mark told her everything except what Romey had said about the body.

An hour after they started Reggie took a break. Clint brought a newspaper and she read the story twice. Then she read her notes again. Mark walked around the office as she read. His lawyer looked very worried, and he nearly felt sorry for her. He really liked her. He sat down again.

'What are you afraid of, Mark?' she said at last.

'Lots of things. I've lied to the police and I think they know it. My little brother's very sick because of me. I haven't told the truth to his doctor either. I don't know what to do, and that's why I'm here. What should I do?'

23

Reggie said thoughtfully, 'Have you told me everything?'

'Almost.'

'Have you lied to me?'

'No.'

'Do you know where the body is?'

'I think so. I know what Jerome Clifford told me.'

'Do you want to tell me where it is?' she asked slowly.

'I'm not sure,' said Mark. 'I'm afraid to tell. I don't want anyone to know that I know about the body. Romey told me his client kills people. He's in the Mafia, and if he thinks I know this secret, he'll want to kill me too. But the cops and the FBI want to talk to me. Do you think I should tell them?'

Reggie stood and walked slowly to the window. She wasn't sure. Mark was safe now, but would he be safe if he told?

'Let's do this, Mark. Don't tell me where the body is. Maybe later, but not now. And let's meet with the FBI and listen to them. You don't have to say a word. I'll do the talking. And after that we'll decide what to do next.'

'Sounds good to me.'

'Okay,' said Reggie. 'Please call your mother and tell her we're coming.' She checked her watch and put more paper in her bag. 'I'm ready,' she said. But she looked nervous.

Chapter 8   The Interview

What Mark saw in the hospital room frightened him at first. Dianne was in the bed, holding Ricky and kissing his head. He was moving and making strange noises. His eyes were open, then shut. 'It's okay, baby,' said Dianne again and again. 'It's okay. Mommy's here. Mommy's here.'

Greenway stood close by. A nurse was on the other side of the bed. No one noticed Mark as he came in. Reggie was waiting outside. It was almost twelve and clearly nobody was thinking of the meeting with the FBI.

Ricky opened his eyes again and seemed to notice his mother. She kissed him again and again, and smiled through her tears.

'He woke up about two hours ago,' the doctor explained. 'But he's not talking yet.'

Mark was glad about that. He didn't want Ricky to start talking about Clifford. Not yet.

'Is he going to be okay?' he asked.

'I think so,' said the doctor. 'But it'll take time. Where's the rest of your family? Your mother needs help.'

'There's only us,' said Mark. 'What about the FBI?'

'She can't talk to them now,' said Greenway. 'But they're waiting for you. They said it's serious.'

'It's okay,' said Mark. 'I'm ready for them. I've got us a lawyer.'

'A lawyer?' said Greenway, surprised. 'How's that?'

'I found her this morning,' said Mark proudly. 'Don't worry. You take care of Ricky and Mom, and me and the lawyer'll take care of the FBI.'

♦

Reggie found an empty room. They were ten minutes late for the meeting, but she wanted to do something first.

'Pull up your shirt,' she said quickly.

She opened her bag and took out a small black recorder. She checked the recorder and tied it to Mark's waist. Mark pulled down his shirt.

'Perfect,' said Reggie. 'Let's go down.'

The meeting was on the second floor, in room 28. Reggie checked the recorder again and turned it on. 'Now go,' she said. 'I'll wait out here. Just remember what I told you.'

◆

Mark took a deep breath and knocked on the door.

'Come in,' someone said. He stepped inside and closed the door. Three men faced him. They were not smiling.

'You must be Mark,' said one. 'Where's your mother?'

'Who are you?' said Mark.

Trumann and McThune introduced themselves. Foltrigg stayed silent. 'Have a seat, Mark,' said Trumann.

'Well Mark, we really wanted to see your mother too.'

'She's with my brother,' said Mark. 'She can't come today. Maybe this can wait until she can come?'

'No Mark, we really need to talk now. Let's talk a few minutes just us and you. Are you nervous?'

'A little,' said Mark. 'What do you want?'

'We want to ask you some questions about yesterday.'

'Do I need a lawyer?'

The detectives looked at each other in surprise. 'Of course not. It's just a few questions, that's all.'

'I already talked to a cop,' said Mark. 'Last night.'

'We're not cops,' said McThune. 'We're FBI.'

'That's why I'm nervous. Maybe I do need a lawyer.'

'What for?'

'To protect my rights.'

The men smiled at each other. 'You've been watching too much TV, kid,' said McThune. 'You don't need a lawyer.'

'Well, can't we wait until my mother can be here?'

They smiled again. 'Not really, Mark. We can wait if we have to, but you're a clever kid and we're in a hurry. We just have a few questions for you.'

'Okay,' said Mark. 'If I have to.'

'Right. First, was Jerome Clifford already dead when you and Ricky found the car yesterday?'

*'Mark, was Jerome Clifford already dead
when you and Ricky found the car?'*

'Do I have to answer the question?'

'Yes. We need to know the truth, Mark.'

'What happens if I don't answer?'

'Oh, lots of things. We could take you down to our office and ask some really hard questions.'

'Could my mother get into trouble?'

'Maybe.'

'What kind of trouble?'

Now the men began to look nervous. They knew they shouldn't talk to children without first talking to their parents. But they kept trying.

'Mark, if a person knows about a crime and doesn't tell the police or the FBI they might be punished. You know, go to prison, or something like that.'

'So if I don't answer your questions, me and Mom might go to prison?'

The men looked at each other again. 'Why don't you want to answer the question, Mark? Are you hiding something?'

'I'm just afraid,' said Mark. 'I'm just eleven years old and you're the FBI, and my Mom's not here.'

Trumann sat forward and looked serious. 'Mark, was Jerome Clifford already dead when you and Ricky found him?'

'I need to go to the bathroom,' said Mark, and got up.

'Okay Mark, take five minutes. We'll wait.'

Mark left the room and closed the door behind him.

◆

The men waited patiently. They knew Mark would talk. But when the door opened again it wasn't Mark. They stood up in surprise.

'Keep your seats,' said the lady who walked in.

'Who are you?' one asked rudely. 'We're in a meeting.'

'I'm Reggie Love,' she said. 'I'm Mark Sway's lawyer.'

The men looked shocked, and sat down again.

'Now,' said Reggie. 'Did you try to talk to my client when his mother wasn't with him?'

'No,' said Trumann.

'He tells me you did.'

'He came here alone,' said McThune quickly. 'We were just having a friendly talk while we waited for her.'

'Did you tell Mark he should talk to a lawyer?'

'We maybe joked about that,' said McThune.

'Mark didn't ask you if he needed a lawyer?'

They shook their heads.

'Did you advise him of his rights?'

'Of course not. He's not a criminal. He's just a kid.'

Reggie slowly opened her bag and took out the black recorder. 'It's all here, boys,' she said. 'Do you want to hear it? You tried to question him without his mother present. You told him he didn't need a lawyer. You didn't tell him his rights, and you said he might go to prison.'

The room was silent.

'Well, boys, from now on I want the truth from you,' she said. 'Now tell me what you want to know from my client.'

They told her.

'I see,' said Reggie. 'You boys really need the body don't you, and you think Mark can help. Well, I'll talk to him some more and I'll meet you in my office around three.'

'Thank you, Ms Love,' said McThune politely.

'It's Reggie,' said Reggie. 'Just call me Reggie.'

Chapter 9   The Reporter

Barry Muldanno was pleased with his new lawyer. He was clever and he was quick. When the lawyer showed him a copy of the Memphis newspaper, Barry went to see his uncle Johnny. Johnny was head of the Mafia in New Orleans, and it was time for Barry to explain a few things. First he explained about the senator's body. Uncle Johnny was not amused. Then he explained about telling Jerome Clifford.

'So what?' said Johnny. 'Clifford's dead now.'

Then Barry explained about the two boys who found him.

'What if Romey told them about the body?' said Barry.

Uncle Johnny became angry. 'You've done a stupid thing, Barry,' he said. 'Now what are you going to do about it?'

'I need to send a killer to Memphis,' said The Blade.

'You're going to kill the boys?' asked his uncle.

'Maybe yes, maybe no,' said Barry. 'First we need to know if they know something.'

'Send Gronke,' said his uncle.

♦

Back in Memphis, Slick Moeller was pleased with his work. The morning newspaper carried his first story about Clifford's death. Now he wanted more news.

Slick walked around the hospital looking for people who would talk to him. He found a cleaner. The cleaner was pleased to talk to a reporter and told him which room the boys were in. He also told him the police had been there.

'The FBI have been here all day too,' said the cleaner. 'And now the family's got a lawyer. Reggie someone. Don't know his other name.'

30

Slick waited near Ricky's room until Mark came out.

'How's your brother?' he asked in a friendly way.

'He's doing great,' said Mark. 'Who are you?'

'I'm a reporter,' said Slick. 'I'm working on a story about Clifford. The cops say you know more about it than you're telling.'

'When's the story coming out?' asked Mark.

'Maybe tomorrow,' said Slick.

Mark felt sick. 'I'm not answering any questions.'

'That's fine,' said Slick, and walked away.

Mark sat down in a quiet corner and began to cry.

♦

Ricky was quiet again. His thumb was back in his mouth, and his eyes were closed. Dianne turned as Mark came into the room.

'Who's this lawyer, Mark?' she asked. 'Why do we need her?'

'I'm frightened, Mom. There are cops all over the place, and the FBI, and now there are reporters wanting to talk to me. We need a lawyer.'

'Lawyers don't work for nothing, Mark.'

'Don't worry, Mom. I paid her a dollar.'

'She's working for a dollar? She must be a great lawyer. What has she done so far?'

'She met the FBI today, and she's meeting them again now. She's coming to talk to you tonight. Mom, I need to tell you some things about me and Ricky.'

And Mark told Dianne what he and Ricky had seen.

'That's why Ricky's in shock,' said Mark. 'Will you explain to Dr Greenway? It might help him to help Ricky.'

'Okay,' said Dianne. 'You've done nothing wrong, trying to help that man. But why did you lie to the doctor?'

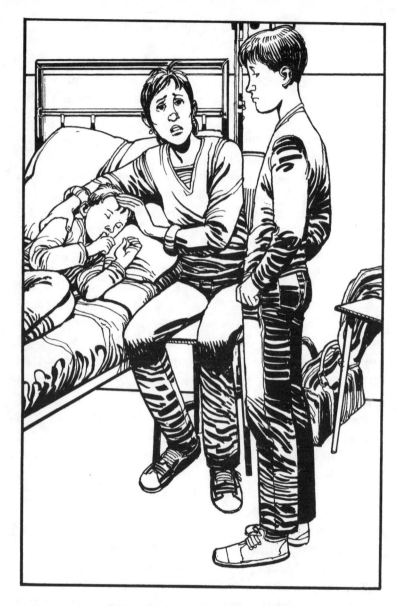

'Who's this lawyer, Mark?' she asked.
'Why do we need her?'

'Tell him I only just remembered,' said Mark. 'Tell him I was in shock too, a bit like Ricky. But now I remember.'

'I'll tell him,' said Dianne.

Chapter 10   The Mafia Arrive

The photos in Wednesday's newspaper were from the Willow Road schoolbook. They were a year old, but they were the best Slick could find. Under the photos were their names. Mark Sway. Ricky Sway. The story told more about Clifford's death, and said Ricky was in shock at St Peter's hospital.

The story also said a lot about Mark – how he called 911 but didn't give his name, about his fingerprints in the car, and about the FBI wanting to talk to him.

'You're famous,' said a nurse, giving Mark the newspaper.

'What is it?' said Mark, suddenly seeing his own face. He read the story slowly. 'This is bad,' he thought. 'Now the Mafia knows where to find me.'

Mark was on his way to the café for breakfast. He gave the paper back and walked to the lift. The door opened and he stepped in. It was empty. It was still early.

At floor number eight the lift stopped and a man stepped in. He wore a white coat and jeans. Mark didn't look at him. He was tired of meeting new people.

The door closed and suddenly the man grabbed Mark. He had a knife. He pushed his horrible face near Mark's.

'Listen to me, Mark Sway,' he said. 'I don't know what Jerome Clifford told you, but if you repeat a single word of it, even to your lawyer, I'll kill you. And I'll kill your mother and your little brother.'

Gronke was doing his job well. Mark was white with fear.

He had a knife. He pushed his horrible face near Mark's.

'I know where you live,' continued the man. 'And I know where you go to school. You can't escape me, understand?'

Mark's eyes were suddenly wet. He nodded yes, yes, yes.

The lift was stopping again. 'And if you tell anyone about me I'll get you,' said the man, and he disappeared.

◆

Reggie reached her office at nine. Clint made her a cup of coffee and gave her the morning newspaper.

'Coffee's excellent,' she said, as she opened the paper and saw Mark's picture. Suddenly Mark himself was in the room, wet from the rain and out of breath.

'What's the matter, Mark?' she asked. 'How's Ricky?'

'He's okay,' said Mark. 'Have you seen today's paper?'

'I've just read it,' she said. 'Does it worry you?'

'Of course it does.'

Clint came into the room with a hot drink for Mark. Mark thanked him and warmed his hands on the cup.

'Are you ready to meet the FBI at ten?' asked Reggie.

'I'm not sure I want to talk to them.'

'Okay, you don't have to. You look frightened. Why?'

'What would happen to me if I never told anyone what I know?'

'You've told me.'

'Yes, but you're my lawyer. And I haven't told you everything – not where the body is.'

'I know, Mark.'

'So what happens if I never tell?'

Reggie had been thinking about this all night, but she still had no answer. Yesterday afternoon, when she met Foltrigg, she saw that he would try everything possible to get Mark to talk. A lie could save Mark. One simple lie. But she was a lawyer and she could not advise him to lie. Poor kid.

'I think they'll try to make you talk,' she said at last. 'It's very rare, but I think the law can make you tell what you know to a judge.'

'And if I refuse?'

'Good question, Mark. If you were an adult, you could go to prison. I don't know what they'd do with a child. But if you lie to the judge you could be in big trouble.'

'If I tell the truth, I'm in bigger trouble.'

'Why?'

Mark didn't answer.

'Mark, at the hospital last night you told me you were ready to talk to the FBI and tell them your story. Now you've changed your mind. Why? What's happened?'

Mark gently put his cup on the table, covered his face and began to cry.

♦

Until ten o'clock, Roy Foltrigg was in an excellent mood. All yesterday afternoon his men had been finding information about Reggie Love. They knew she used to be married to a rich doctor. They knew the doctor had left her. And they knew that she had started drinking heavily and taking drugs, so the doctor was able to take her children from her. Now she had no husband, no children and no money. And a new name. Roy Foltrigg thought he could use this information against Reggie.

Foltrigg's job was to prove that Barry Muldanno had killed the senator. He was sure that Mark knew something that would help him. Then he would win the case, and have his face on the front pages of the newspapers again.

At ten o'clock Foltrigg returned to Reggie's office, ready for the promised meeting with Mark. Clint opened the door to him.

'I'm sorry, Mr Foltrigg,' he said. 'Reggie and Mark have nothing to discuss today.'

Foltrigg shouted angrily, then left, banging the door. He went straight to the FBI office and shouted some more.

'I want the kid followed,' he said angrily. 'We know Gronke's in town. He mustn't get to the kid. Watch the lawyer too. And I want you to prepare papers to take to a judge. We're going to make Mark Sway talk.'

Chapter 11   Momma Love

When Reggie and Mark returned to the hospital there were reporters everywhere.

'Ms Love, Ms Love,' they called. 'Just a few questions, please.' She took Mark's hand and walked faster.

'Is it true your client is refusing to speak to the FBI? Did your client talk to Jerome Clifford before he died? Is it true your client knows where the senator's body is?'

Reggie said quickly to Mark, 'Don't look at them and don't say a word.'

In room 943 Ricky was sitting on the end of the bed. Dr Greenway told Mark to sit next to him and hold his hand.

'Ricky,' he said, 'I would like to talk about the other day when you and Mark were hiding in the trees.'

'It's okay, Ricky,' said Mark. 'He knows we were smoking. Mom's not angry with us.'

'I'm really cold,' said Ricky.

'Ricky, it's very warm in here,' said Dr Greenway. 'Now do you remember seeing the big black car?'

'Yes,' said Ricky quietly.

'What did the big black car do, Ricky?'

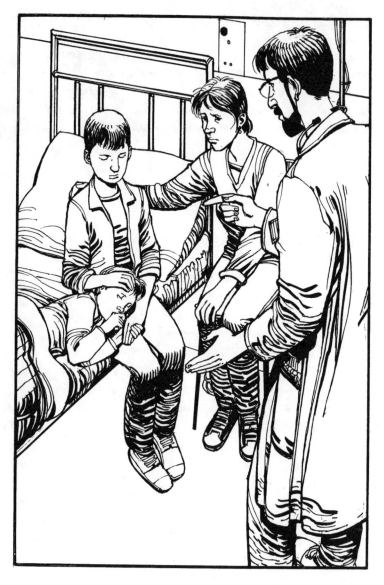

*Ricky shut his eyes tightly, put his head on Mark's knee
and his thumb went into his mouth. He didn't speak
another word for twenty-four hours.*

Ricky shut his eyes tightly, put his head on Mark's knee and his thumb went into his mouth. He didn't speak another word for twenty-four hours.

♦

Reggie asked Dianne if Mark could spend the night at her house. Dianne agreed, so when Ricky was asleep again they left the hospital in Reggie's sports car. It was old, but Reggie liked to drive fast, and that was fine with Mark.

Mark watched the mirror closely to see if anyone was following them.

'You think Mom and Ricky are safe?' he asked.

'Yes. Don't worry about them. The hospital promised to keep guards at the door. Now I wonder what Momma Love is giving us for dinner?'

Momma Love was Reggie's mother. She often had young guests to dinner. Most of Reggie's work was with children. Some had family problems, some had drug problems and some had already started a life of crime. Reggie often decided that they needed good food at Momma Love's.

'Momma Love's cooking is the best,' she told Mark.

And it was. Momma Love was half Italian, and she cooked food the old way. Everything was fresh and smelled perfect. They spent an hour at the table, talking and eating. Dinner in the trailer never took more than ten minutes!

After dinner Momma Love showed Mark some photographs. 'Reggie's children,' she said. 'I never see them now. One's on drugs and the other has big money problems. Their father took them and spoiled them. Reggie felt angry at first, but she's got a new life now and tries not to think about it.'

Mark's bed was comfortable, and he fell asleep quickly, but around two o'clock he woke up and found himself worrying about Mom and Ricky. Why was he here? His place was with them, at the hospital. He got up and stood at the window, thinking about the past two days. It had all started on Monday, after school. Now he had missed two days of school. When would it all end?

As Mark looked into the dark night he suddenly noticed a small red light. A cigarette. Someone was out there, in the street, smoking a cigarette. Though he couldn't be seen, Mark held his breath. Someone was watching the house.

♦

Gronke put out his cigarette and went to his car. The kid was not going to move tonight, and he had something to do. He drove to Tucker Trailer Park.

Chapter 12   Things Get Worse

Seven-thirty a.m. was too early for Reggie, but she had to get Mark back to Dianne. Clint called before they left.

'Bad news, Reggie,' he said. 'Mark's picture is on the front page again. Slick Moeller has written another story.'

When they got to the hospital they could see the reporters waiting outside the front door.

'Follow me,' said Mark, and led Reggie through a side door to the kitchens and up the back stairs. 'I know this hospital well now, don't I?' he said proudly.

His smile dropped when he saw his mother. She was sitting in the hall with a cop next to her. She was crying hard. Mark ran to her. She grabbed him and held him tight.

'Mark,' she said. 'Our trailer burned down last night.'

'That's right,' said the cop. 'Just a few hours ago.'

Dianne was still crying. 'Everything's gone, Mark.'

'What started the fire?' Reggie asked.

'Don't know yet,' said the cop.

'How's Ricky, Mom?' asked Mark.

'He's okay,' said Dianne. 'He had a good night.'

'Look Mom,' said Mark, 'can we go inside and talk?'

Dianne nodded and took him into the room. When the door closed, the tiny, homeless Sway family was all alone.

♦

Foltrigg had a plan. 'Maybe we can get a judge to take Mark into custody. Get the law to keep him safe for us.'

The others looked interested.

'Here are the advantages,' said Foltrigg. 'First, it will protect Mark from the Mafia. At the same time, it will frighten Mark and make him ready to talk. We'll tell the judge we need Mark safe so he can talk in court.'

'If you want to do that,' said McThune, 'you need to see Judge Harry Roosevelt. He's the chief judge for the children's courts here in Memphis. But don't tell him you want to frighten Mark. The best way to get him to agree to custody is to show him that Mark is in danger. And if you want to get Mark into court you will have to say he knows something that will help the Muldanno case.'

'He knows something all right,' said Foltrigg. 'I'm sure of it.'

♦

When Judge Harry Roosevelt became a judge twenty-two years ago, he was the first black judge of the children's court in Tennessee. He was clever, he was kind, and he was wise. When he heard about the danger to Mark Sway he thought carefully. He didn't like to do it, but he agreed to hear Mark in court, and to take him into custody until then.

He signed an order. 'Take him into the children's prison,' he said.

'Give him a private room. Do not frighten him. I'll speak to his lawyer later today.'

♦

Mark and Dianne were in their room talking about the fire and all the things they had lost. They whispered because they didn't want Ricky to know about the fire yet.

Ricky was awake. His eyes were open but he was staring at the ceiling without saying a word or moving at all.

There was something Mark didn't say to Dianne. Something that worried him. Maybe the fire wasn't an accident. Could it be another message from the man with the knife? Trailers didn't usually burn down at four o'clock in the morning.

There was a knock at the door. Mark opened it.

Two men entered the room. 'Memphis Police here. Detective Nassar and Detective Klickman. Looking for Dianne Sway.' And they handed Dianne some papers.

'These are from the children's court, Ms Sway,' said Nassar. 'We're here to take Mark Sway into custody now, ma'am. The judge wants to see him in court this afternoon.'

'What!' Dianne shouted at Nassar, dropping the papers.

'Judge's orders,' said Nassar, picking up the papers.

'You can't take my son,' shouted Dianne.

But they could, and they did, pulling him into the hall. Dianne ran after them, grabbed Mark and screamed. Nassar held Dianne and Klickman tried to pull Mark away. Dianne kicked Klickman and there was more screaming and fighting.

In the middle of all this, Ricky appeared at the door. He stared at Mark, who was held by Klickman. He stared at his mother, who was held by Nassar. Everyone stared at Ricky. His face was white and his mouth was open.

'It's okay, Mom, I'll go,' said Mark. 'Look after Ricky. And call Reggie. Tell her to come to the prison.'

♦

A lady in a uniform with DOREEN on the pocket met them at the prison. She gave Nassar a paper to sign and asked Mark to empty his pockets. Everything went into a metal box. Then she took him to a small room. It wasn't too bad, but Mark felt very lonely.

'Can I use a phone?' he asked. 'To call my Mom?'

Doreen brought him a phone and a phone book. 'You can have it for ten minutes,' she said, and locked the door.

Mark found the number for St Peter's and asked for room 943. 'Number 943 isn't taking calls just now,' he was told. Ricky must be asleep, thought Mark. He tried Reggie. No luck. Then he had an idea. He called a pizza restaurant.

'This is Detective Klickman, Memphis Police,' he said in a deep voice. 'Please send me forty pizzas for a surprise party here in the police station. I'll pay when they come.'

When Doreen came back for the phone, Mark looked much happier.

Chapter 13   Back to Prison

Reggie didn't hear about Mark until lunchtime on Thursday. She often worked in the children's courts, and she knew Judge Roosevelt well. She rushed to his office.

'I'm not surprised to see you, Reggie,' he said.

'I can't understand why you did this, Harry,' she said. 'Mark has done nothing wrong.'

'I've agreed to see him in court this afternoon,' said the judge, 'and I'm keeping him safe until then. Wait here. I'll ask the guards to bring him here to see you now.'

When Mark arrived he smiled at Reggie. 'Don't worry,' he said, 'I'm okay. But what should I say in court?'

43

'No one can make you talk,' she said,
'but the judge can keep you in custody if you don't.'

Reggie explained carefully. 'No one can make you talk,' she said, 'but the judge can keep you in custody if you don't.'

'But I've done nothing wrong.'

'No,' said Reggie, 'but if the judge asks you questions and you don't answer, then that would be wrong. The law is very clear on this. If you know something that will help a murder case, you can't keep quiet, even if you think you're in danger.'

'It's a stupid law,' said Mark.

'Maybe,' said Reggie, 'but we can't change it today.'

'I could tell them I don't know anything,' said Mark.

Reggie wanted to say yes, but she kept silent. At last she said firmly, 'You can't lie in court, Mark.'

♦

Slick Moeller was waiting outside the courtroom. He saw Mark go in with two guards. He saw Reggie go in next, and then the FBI men, with Foltrigg. He smiled to himself. In the children's court there could be no cameras and no reporters. He knew Foltrigg wouldn't like that!

The courtroom door was locked and Slick waited patiently. When it was unlocked again he walked quickly into the men's toilets and waited there. Soon one of the guards joined him.

'What happened?' asked Slick. 'Be quick.'

'The kid wouldn't talk,' said the guard, 'so he's going back to prison.'

'What does he know?'

'The judge asked him if he knew where the senator's body is, but he wouldn't answer.'

'What next?' asked Slick.

'The judge wants to see him again tomorrow. He's given him one night to change his mind.'

Slick passed the guard one hundred dollars.

They wanted to explain how the government could protect Mark and his family if he gave evidence against the Mafia.

'You didn't hear it from me,' said the guard.

'Trust me,' said Slick.

♦

Foltrigg was shouting again. 'That no-good judge,' he said again and again. 'That no-good judge. He's too soft. I'm going back to New Orleans. This murder case is a New Orleans job. I can get Mark called to the courts in New Orleans. Then we can really make him talk.'

♦

But the FBI had other ideas. When Foltrigg had left they asked for another meeting with the judge and Reggie. They wanted to explain how the government could protect Mark and his family if he gave evidence against the Mafia.

'It's called the witness protection programme,' said McThune.

'I've heard of it, Mr McThune,' said the judge. 'Tell us more about it.'

'It's quite simple. We move the family to another city. We give them new names. We find a good job for the mother, and get them a nice place to live. We make sure the boys are in a good school. We give them some money. And we stay close by.'

'Well, Reggie?' said the judge. 'It sounds good.'

It certainly did. At the moment the Sways had no home. Dianne had a poor job. They had no relations in Memphis.

'They can't move just now,' she said. 'Ricky must stay in hospital.'

'We've found a children's hospital in Phoenix that can take him right away,' said McThune. 'It's a private hospital, and of course we'll pay for it.'

'What do you think, Reggie?' asked Judge Roosevelt.

'I'll talk to Dianne about it,' said Reggie.

'Good,' said the judge. 'And see if she can come to court tomorrow. I'd like her to be there.'

'I'll try,' said Reggie.

♦

Mark was also thinking about how to save his family. Doreen was surprised to see him back at the prison.

'How long are you back for?' she asked.

'The judge didn't say. I have to go to court again tomorrow.'

'How's your little brother?'

Mark put on a very sad face. 'He's probably going to die,' he said.

'No!'

'Yes,' said Mark in a small voice. 'He doesn't talk. He makes terrible noises. And he doesn't eat.'

'I'm sorry.'

'It's bad. I don't feel so good myself.'

'Poor kid. Anything I can get you?'

'No, I just need to lie down.'

'Poor kid,' she said again. 'I'll keep an eye on you.'

Chapter 14   No Other Way

Slick's story of Mark's courtroom appearance was in the newspaper on Friday morning – front page news again. Gronke took the first plane to New Orleans and called The Blade.

'Look, Barry,' he said. 'I can't do much when the kid's in prison, can I? But he hasn't talked yet. Think about it. I got to him with a knife. I burned the trailer. The kid's too frightened to speak.'

'I don't know, Gronke,' said Muldanno. 'The kid knows something. Sure you can't get to him?'

'We can't kill the kid, Barry. Everyone's watching him.'

'What about his mother or brother?'

Gronke said nothing. He was tired of Muldanno's game.

'What about his lawyer?'

'Why do you want to kill his lawyer?'

'Because I hate lawyers,' said The Blade wildly.

'No, Barry,' said Gronke, wondering if Muldanno was going mad. 'I'm not in the mood to kill anyone just now.'

'That's fine,' said Muldanno. 'Another man can do it.'

♦

When Judge Roosevelt read Slick's story his eyes grew cold. In the children's court everything was private. How did Moeller get his information? He would call Moeller to the court today to explain. It was going to be another busy day, but at the end of it his sons would take him fishing for the weekend. He smiled at this pleasant thought.

♦

The courtroom story made Foltrigg angry again. But the papers to call Mark to the court in New Orleans were nearly ready. He took a call from the local FBI.

'Mr Foltrigg, we thought you'd like to know that Gronke's back in town. He arrived this morning. And we have a recording of a phone conversation with Muldanno.'

'Let me hear it,' said Foltrigg.

'Good,' he said when he'd heard it. 'Send it to Memphis. I want Judge Roosevelt to hear it today. It will make him keep Mark Sway in custody for the weekend. Tonight we'll send papers to call Mark to New Orleans. The courts are closed until Monday, and by that time we'll have the kid here where we want him.'

♦

Slick's story made Reggie sad. With newspaper reports like this, the Mafia knew everything that was going on.

She sat with Mark now, trying to explain about the witness protection programme.

'What does Mom think?' asked Mark.

'She's not sure,' said Reggie.

'I'm not sure either,' said Mark. 'I saw this once in a film. Someone told the truth about the Mafia and the FBI helped him to disappear. He got a new face, even a new wife. He went to Brazil.'

'What happened?'

'It took the Mafia a year to find him. They killed his wife too.'

'It was just a film, Mark. There's no other way. It's the safest thing to do.'

'Of course I have to tell them what I know before they'll do all these wonderful things for us.'

'That's part of the agreement, Mark.'

'The Mafia never forgets, Reggie.'

'You've watched too many films, Mark.'

'It's easy for you, Reggie. You'll be fine. But we'll live in fear for the rest of our lives.'

'There's no other way, Mark.'

'Yes there is. I could lie.'

Chapter 15   Escape!

Mark didn't lie, but he wasn't ready yet to tell the truth. When the court met again on Friday afternoon, no one was really surprised when he again refused to answer the judge's questions. 'I'm not going to answer that,' he said, time after time.

But everyone was shocked by the recording that was played. Reggie's eyes opened wide when she heard Muldanno speak of killing her. The judge agreed that Mark was in great danger, and returned him to custody.

There was a surprise, though, when Slick Moeller came before the judge. True to his word, the reporter refused to name the person who gave him private information.

'Well Mr Moeller,' said the judge. 'If I can send a child to prison for refusing to tell what he knows, I can do the same for you.'

Slick knew more than anyone about crime in Memphis, but he had never been inside a prison. Now it was his turn.

♦

'Well Mr Moeller,' said the judge. 'If I can send a child to prison
for refusing to tell what he knows, I can do the same for you.'

Back in his prison room, Mark was ready for his plan. For half an hour he ran around his room, until his heart was going very fast and his face was red and hot. When he heard Doreen's key he lay on the floor, closed his eyes, and put his thumb in his mouth.

'Mark,' shouted Doreen, when she saw him. 'Mark – oh you poor kid!' She ran from the room to get help, and was back in a few seconds with another guard.

'Mark was worried about this,' said Doreen. 'He's in shock like his little brother. Look – his skin is all wet. And his heart is going so fast!'

'Stay here. I'll call an ambulance,' said the other guard. 'We need to get him to hospital.'

Everything was confused after that. Nobody wanted a boy to die in prison. When the ambulance came the guards signed papers to send Mark to hospital and he was taken at once to St Peter's. More papers. There were nurses everywhere, and everyone was in a hurry. A nurse moved Mark to a bed.

'Sign this,' said the ambulance men, 'and be quick. We have another case waiting.'

The nurse signed, the men left, and the nurse went to answer a phone. Mark opened his eyes and saw he was alone. He jumped off the bed and ran into a hall. Nobody noticed him. He disappeared into an empty office and found a phone.

'Reggie?' he said quickly when she answered the phone. 'I'm in St Peter's. I can't talk now. Please come and get me. Don't tell anyone. I'll be in the car park.'

Mark knew how to hide in the hospital. He moved quickly and quietly, and found his way to the car park. When Reggie's car arrived he climbed in and hid on the floor.

'Drive, Reggie,' he said. 'Drive anywhere. Let's go. I'll explain later.'

◆

When the nurse came back, Mark was not there. 'Someone's moved him,' she thought, and hurried off to another job.

When Foltrigg's men arrived with papers to take Mark to New Orleans they checked the prison, and then checked the hospital. Only then did people realise that he was gone.

'He's what?' cried Dianne.

'Go find him,' said McThune.

But by then Mark and Reggie were on the road.

'Where are we going?' asked Reggie.

'Listen, Reggie,' said Mark. 'I've been thinking. What if Romey told me a lie? What if the body isn't where he said? Then I'd be safe. We need to check. We need to go to New Orleans.'

Chapter 16   New Orleans

On Saturday the news was out. Everyone was looking for Mark. When Barry Muldanno heard, he was wild with fear. He went straight to tell his uncle.

'The kid's disappeared,' he said. 'What's he going to do now? I need to move the body. Help me. Give me two men.'

'You're stupid, stupid, stupid,' said Uncle Johnny. 'I'll give you two men, but don't get caught.'

'I'll do it tonight,' said Barry, 'when it's dark.'

♦

Reggie and Mark reached New Orleans on Saturday afternoon. They drove all night, stopping only to sleep a few hours in the car. Reggie knew it was wrong. She knew the cops and the FBI would be looking for them.

They talked through the night, about Memphis and Mark's life there, about his school and his friends. Then Mark said sadly, 'If the body *is* there, I can't go back to Memphis, can I?' So they talked about the witness protection plan.

Reggie still had no idea where they were going.

'We have to find Clifford's house,' said Mark.

'The body's there? Are you crazy?'

'It's there,' said Mark, 'under his boat in the garage.'

They found the house late on Saturday afternoon. The streets were quiet, so they parked the car and walked round to the back of the house. All was silent.

'There's the garage,' said Mark quietly.

'This is crazy,' said Reggie. 'We'll wait until dark.'

♦

Reggie looked at her watch. Midnight. They were hiding in the tall grass behind the house. She was tired and had pains in her legs. It was time to move.

Slowly they crawled through the grass towards the garage. Reggie was shaking. She was afraid of snakes. Suddenly Mark stopped. 'There's a light in there,' he whispered. 'There's someone there. Stay here Reggie.'

He crawled silently to a window. There was the boat. And it was moving. He saw the shapes of three men.

'Okay, Muldanno,' said one of the men. 'Where do we dig?'

Mark's heart was in his mouth. He crawled back to Reggie. 'It's Muldanno,' he whispered. 'They're digging up the body. What do we do now?'

'Oh no!' said Reggie. 'I told you this was crazy. Let me think.' And suddenly she knew what to do.

She crawled in the other direction, towards the house next door. With her shoe she broke a window. Suddenly the night was no longer silent. Bells rang everywhere. Lights went on in the house next door. Voices were shouting. A man appeared with a gun. He shot wildly into the dark.

'Look,' called Mark, 'they're leaving.' Muldanno and his men ran out of the garage and disappeared. Reggie crawled back.

It was another hour before the confusion ended. Police came to the house next door. More shouting, more lights. Mark and Reggie stayed hidden behind Clifford's garage. Then all was silent again.

'Come on,' said Mark. 'We have to look.'

The lock on the garage door was broken. In the dark, they moved towards the boat. Next to it there was a hole. In the hole was a plastic bag.

'We have to look,' said Mark again. And they opened the bag. The horrible, dead face of the senator stared up at them. The smell was terrible.

Reggie felt sick, but now they knew the truth.

'Come on,' she said, 'I have to make a phone call.'

Chapter 17   Waiting

It was Sunday morning. Everyone was waiting.

In Johnny's office, Muldanno was waiting nervously for night to come. He would have to try again.

At his home, Foltrigg was waiting angrily for news of Mark. He needed him in court on Monday.

At the city airport, Mark and Reggie were waiting. They were in a private room with Detective Trumann of the FBI.

'What time will they be here?' asked Reggie.

'Soon,' said Trumann. 'They left an hour ago.'

'Will they have the papers?' asked Reggie.

'Sure,' said Trumann. 'Everything you asked for.'

Mark was at a window, watching a jet take off. He thought he would like flying. Maybe he would be a pilot.

'He's a brave kid,' said Trumann to Reggie.

A black FBI jet landed. 'Is it them?' Mark asked excitedly. The door opened, the stairs came down, and McThune appeared. He was followed by Dianne, then Dr Greenway carrying Ricky. Trumann led Mark and Reggie to meet them.

Reggie watched while Mark and Dianne held each other close. Then she turned to McThune.

'You'll take Ricky to a hospital?' she asked.

'Agreed. We have a room booked in Phoenix. A private hospital. They're waiting for Ricky.'

'When he's better they can choose where to live?'

'Agreed,' said McThune. 'It's all in the papers. I just need you and Ms Sway to sign.'

'Mom,' said Mark. 'I've been thinking. What about Australia? They have real cowboys there. I saw it in a film once.'

'No more films for you, Mark,' laughed Dianne. 'No more TV. Just books from now on.' And she signed the papers.

Reggie watched as Mark and Dianne walked back to the plane. Suddenly Mark turned.

'Aren't you coming, Reggie?' he asked.

'No, Mark. I can't.'

He bit his lip. 'I'll never see you again, will I?'

She shook her head. There were tears in her eyes.

'I love you Mark. I'll miss you.'

'I'll miss you too,' he said, and for once he was not ashamed to cry in public.

'I'll never see you again,' said Mark again, almost to himself. He dried his wet eyes with the back of his hand and walked slowly to join his mother. At the top of the stairs he turned for one last look.

♦

Minutes later as the plane moved away, Trumann said again, 'He's a brave kid.'

Reggie looked at the plane and said nothing. Then she turned and told him what he wanted to know.

'The body is in the garage behind Jerome Clifford's house,' she said. '886 East Brookline.'

'Thanks, Reggie,' Trumann said, suddenly ready to leave.

'Don't thank me,' said Reggie, looking into the clouds. 'Thank Mark.'

ACTIVITIES

Chapters 1–3

Before you read

1 Look at the picture on the front of the book.

   a What do you think is the relationship between the three people?

   b How would you describe each person's mood, from this picture? Choose from these words:

   angry anxious bored cruel dangerous
   frightened happy nasty pleasant sad

2 Check these words in your dictionary.

   client evidence fingerprints trial trust

   Choose the best words to complete these sentences:

   a The murder . . . . . was reported in all the newspapers.

   b The police had . . . . . that the woman was driving the car.

   c She . . . . . her best friend with the secret.

   d They took her . . . . . off the door handle.

   e She was a very good lawyer, so her . . . . . were happy to pay her a lot of money.

3 Now check these words:

   crawl grab tail pipe trailer

   Which word is . . .

   a . . . a house on wheels?

   b . . . a way of moving on your stomach so people won't see you?

   c . . . a way of taking something from another person quickly and rudely?

   d . . . part of a car. It is at the back and it takes gas away from the car engine.

After you read

4 Answer these questions:

   a How does Romey try to kill himself?

   b Where is the body of the senator?

   c Who is Barry Muldano?

5 Work with two other students. Dianne comes home from work and

finds Ricky in shock. What do you think happens when the doctor arrives? Act out the scene between Dianne, the doctor and Mark.

Student A: You are Diane.   *Student C*: You are Mark.
Student B: You are the doctor.

Chapters 4–6

Before you read

6 Do you think Mark will tell the FBI men the truth when they check his fingerprints?
7 Will Slick become a friend to Mark? How could he help Mark?
8 What do you think Barry will do next?
9 Find the word *truth* in your dictionary. Now write a sentence with *truth* in it, to show the meaning clearly.

After you read

10 Answer these questions.
    a Why is Gill Teal talking to the man in the wheelchair?
    b What do the FBI tell Foltrigg about Mark?
    c How does Mark find Reggie?
11 Work with two other students. McThune and Trumann need Dr Greenway's permission before they can talk to Ricky. What do you think they will say to each other when they ask for permission? Act out the conversation between them.

Student A: You are McThune.   *Student C*: You are Dr Greenway.
Student B: You are Trumann.

Chapters 7–9

Before you read

12 What do you think will happen at twelve when Mark talks to the FBI?
13 What do you think will happen next at the hospital?
14 Check the word *rights* in your dictionary.
    Put the words *interviewed/police/rights* in the spaces in this sentence:
    In most countries, people have certain . . . . . when they are . . . . . by the . . . . . .

After you read

15 Answer these questions:
  a What does Mark tell Reggie about his family?
  b What does Mark tell Reggie about Romey?
  c What doesn't Mark tell Reggie?

16 Why doesn't Dianne go to talk to the FBI with Mark?

17 What does Reggie do to stop the FBI's questions?

18 Who does Barry Muldanno go to for help?

19 Whose idea is it to send Gronke to Memphis?

20 At the hospital Mark tells his mother more about what he and Ricky had seen. Why does he decide to tell her then?

21 Reggie doesn't go to the interview with Mark. Instead, she puts the recorder on him. What are the advantages of doing this? Can you think of another plan she could have tried?
  Discuss with other students.

Chapters 10–13

Before you read

22 Look at the picture on page 34. Who do you think the man is? What do you think he is saying to Mark?

23 If you were Mark, what would you say now to Slick Moeller? Or would you say nothing?

24 Check the word *custody* in your dictionary.
  Make a sentence using this group of words:
  police/thief/custody/prison

After you read

25 Answer these questions:
  a What does Gronke do to Mark?
  b What does Reggie think the FBI will try to do?
  c What do you know about Reggie's family?
  d How does Mark know they were followed to Momma Love's house?
  e What is a witness protection programme?

26 With another student, act the conversation at the police station between Detective Klickman and the pizza delivery man.

Student A: You are Detective Klickman.
Student B: You are the pizza delivery man.

Chapters 14–17

Before you read

27 How do you think Mark can help his family? What do you think his plan is?

28 Do you think Dianne will agree to the witness protection programme? Why, or why not?

29 What will happen if Mark is called to the courts in New Orleans?

After you read

30 Answer these questions:
  a How does Mark escape from prison?
  b Why does Mark want to go to New Orleans?
  c Why does Reggie keep the secret until Mark has gone?

31 Who says these things?
  a 'The Mafia never forgets, Reggie.'
  b 'I'll give you two men, but don't get caught.'
  c 'No more films for you, Mark.'

Writing

32 After the Sways go to Australia, Mark writes a secret letter to Reggie. What does he say? Write his letter.

33 There were three main people or groups of people interested in the senator's body: the Mafia in New Orleans, the US Government lawyer from New Orleans and the FBI in Memphis. Explain why each one was interested. Who had most to win and who had most to lose by finding the body?

34 Which parts of this story do you find most exciting and why? Is there any part of the story that you would like to change? How would you change it?

Answers for the activities in this book are available from your local Pearson Education office or contact: Penguin Readers Marketing Department, Pearson Education, Edinburgh Gate, Harlow, Essex, CM20 2JE.